Hundreds of years ago in Japan, martial arts weren't sports. They were for real. People fought to defend themselves against bandits and robbers. The techniques of martial arts were used by bandits and robbers to attack and kill.

Samurai warrior

The Japanese practised other martial arts as well. The famous Samurai warriors had a special kind of wrestling, called **sumo wrestling**. Sumo wrestling is very popular in Japan. It has also become popular in other countries.

How karate began

Nobody knows where karate began. Some people think it began in China. Hundreds of years ago, Chinese monks needed to defend themselves against bandits. One of their leaders invented karate, a new way of fighting.

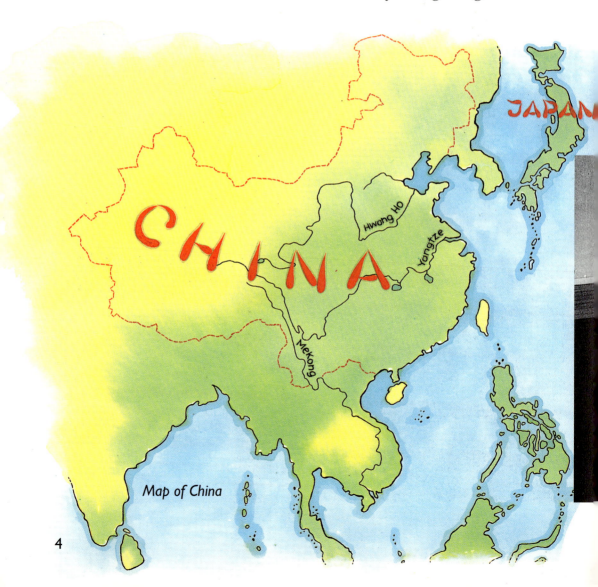

Map of China

What are martial arts?

Most of the martial arts have come to Europe from Japan. The most famous ones are **karate** and **judo**.

Judo

So what's the difference between a martial art and a fight in the street?
Well, there are rules in martial arts.

Karate

Rules of martial arts
• You wear special clothes.
• You do them in a special place.
• You don't fight someone because you hate them and want to hurt them.
• You fight someone because you want to get more points.

Martial arts are a sport.

Hundreds of years later, the martial art of karate came to Japan. The Japanese didn't like it at first. They had their own martial arts, called **ju-jitsu** and **ken-jitsu.** It was only in 1933 that the Japanese accepted the new sport.

The karate masters knew that karate meant 'Chinese hand', but they said it meant 'empty hand'.

They said karate meant 'empty hand' because people fought with their bare hands. The name also showed the thinking behind karate. If you hold on to anything too tightly or too long, you will lose it.

The start of a ju-jitsu game

Starting karate

Jon is 14.
He is a karate
beginner.

*I went to karate
because my friend
does. He goes with
his sister. Our
karate club is at the sports centre.
It's on for two hours on a Monday
night. I said I'd go to watch. When
I got there, the instructor said,
'Have a go.'*

Gi

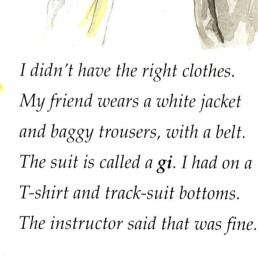

*I didn't have the right clothes.
My friend wears a white jacket
and baggy trousers, with a belt.
The suit is called a **gi**. I had on a
T-shirt and track-suit bottoms.
The instructor said that was fine.*

Everyone was barefoot
so I had to take my
shoes off.

The instructor clapped his hands.
He shouted at everyone to get
ready to start. He told
me to go over to the beginners'
group. My friend and his sister
were in the middle group.

They were both wearing red belts.
The ones on my side had white
belts. Three of them were wearing
ordinary clothes, like me.

7

I thought you'd start kicking and fighting right away. It wasn't like that at all. We spent more than half an hour doing exercises.

At first I thought it was really easy. But when it came to some twisting and stretching, that was really difficult.

I was tired out after all that, but the instructor didn't give us a break. He lined us all up, and we had to stand with legs apart and our hands in fists. Then everybody bowed.

After that one of the men from the top group came over to us. He was a senior. He gave us a movement to do. It wasn't difficult, just moving forward with a big step.

Then he showed us a hand movement to do as well.

Then we had to do both movements together. Next we had to hold our arms up in front of our faces.

Then we had to do all three movements in one go. It sounds easy, but we were all over the place. We all had to move at the same time. Some people started with the wrong foot. Other people moved too quickly, and bumped into the people in front.

I looked at the other groups. They were working in a line and they were all doing the same moves. They moved very quickly and you could hardly see what they were doing.

They moved forward – the ones in the top group were doing kicks as well. Then they punched their fists forward, and gave a great shout.

At the end of the session my
friend came over to me.

'Did you enjoy it?'

'You bet, but I'm aching
all over! Does it get
easier next time?'

'The exercises get easier.
You also learn new movements
in each lesson. Why don't you
come next week, at the same
time?'

'See you then.'

Rules

Karate is a fighting sport and it can be dangerous. Rules and good manners help to stop people getting hurt. The rules and manners about how to behave were set up very long ago. They are a part of the Japanese way of life.

Japanese people bow to each other when they meet

This is the **dojo**. The dojo is the place where you do karate. When you come through the door of the dojo, the first thing you do is take your shoes off. Then you bow, and say '**Osu'.** This sounds like O-ss.

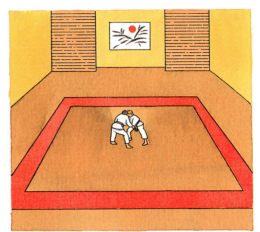

Osu
Comes from osu-shinobu.
This was a Samurai greeting.

When the students are lined up, ready to start the lesson, they stand in a special way. Then the students and teacher bow.

13

More about karate

What weapons do you use in karate?

The basic weapons of modern karate are parts of our body.

What is the karate chop?

The **karate chop** is the knife-hand. This is the karate move you always see in films and on TV.

What other hand movements are there?

The first you learn is the **seiken**, the fist. You strike with the first two knuckles.

This is the **shotei**, the palm hand. You strike with the lower part of the palm.

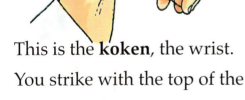

This is the **keikio**, the chicken beak. You strike with the finger tips.

This is the **koken**, the wrist. You strike with the top of the wrist.

Is there a knife-foot?
Yes. It's called **sokuto**. You strike with the outside of the foot.

Which is the most important of all the moves?
All teachers say the **seiken** is very important.

First, you learn how to make the fist. Then you learn how to give a blow with it. It takes six to nine months to learn this. Then you can begin to use the **makiwari**. This is a kind of punching post.

makiwari

seiken

Kata

In karate, a **kata** is a group of exercises which you do in a fixed order.

Every kata begins with a defensive blocking technique. This is because karate is more about self-defence than attack.

You learn each kata in three stages.

1. Each technique of the kata has to be learnt. You work on each technique separately. Then you learn the next technique and then you practise them together. Now you add the next technique. This usually takes about a month.

Kata are an important part of all karate training. You also use kata when you are fighting.

2. Then you put it all together, and work on any weak moves. You need to get the timing right.

3. Finally, you have to understand how to apply what you have learnt.

While you are working on a kata, you can only think about the movements you are doing. Unless you do this, you won't have control and your timing won't be right.

Breathing and relaxing

Breathing is very important in karate. Most people don't breathe very well. We take quick, shallow breaths when we are worried or nervous. You can learn to control your breathing and to put aside your worries and nerves. This is all part of karate training.

tameshiwar

Tameshiwar is a Japanese word. It means 'destruction'. This is the art of using your bare hand or foot to smash a brick, or a plank of a wood.

Ben and Dave are both Black Belts at karate. They are giving a demonstration of tameshiwar skills. They have to break a brick with the side of the hand.

Ben goes first. He hasn't had his Black Belt long. He knows a lot of people are watching. He starts thinking about them, rather than about breaking the brick.

Ben starts to build up his blocks to support the bricks. He worries about them. Is he building them up properly? Will they fall down?

Ben is feeling nervous. His ▶ breathing isn't controlled, and that makes him feel even worse. When he tries to break the brick, he can't do anything.

◀ Dave remembers feeling like Ben when he was first a Black Belt. He doesn't worry any more about the people watching. Instead, he starts by working on his breathing. He comes on, and bows.

Then, without hurrying or ▶ feeling nervous, he builds up his blocks and bricks. His breathing is even. He lets out a shout as he strikes the brick. The brick breaks.

21

Contests

A lot of karate is done by each person on their own. You have to learn the kata by yourself. But karate is also about fighting an opponent. This is called sparring, and the Japanese word for it is **kumite.**

When you learn kumite, you begin working with, not against, your partner. As you get better, you can do free sparring.

kumite

Free-fighting kumite is the most exciting kind of match to watch. Each match is controlled by a referee and a 'shadow' referee. They move around the mat with the fighters. They try to see exactly what each fighter is doing.

23

Fighters can strike to the face, neck, chest, body, stomach and back. A fighter wins points for technique, not for hitting the other fighter. A full point, is given when the technique is exactly right. This is called an **ippon**. The attacker tries to get the moves and timing exactly right.

ippon
A full point in a
karate match

Half points are given for techniques which are nearly perfect. The top score in a contest is six half-points.

The referees are strict. They give half-point or full-point penalties for breaking the rules.

Some competitions allow 'contact-karate', where the fighters are allowed to kick and hit each other. Many karate instructors don't like this. They say that karate is about control and strength, and should not be a violent sport.

How judo began

Judo was started by Jigoro Kano. Kano was Japanese. He lived more than 100 years ago. He was worried that Japanese schoolchildren didn't do enough exercise.

Kano brought the old fighting system of ju-jitsu up to date. His new system was called Kodokan judo. This is the sport which millions of people all round the world do today. It has even become an Olympic sport.

Many of the techniques of modern judo come from the old martial art of ju-jitsu. Ju-jitsu was a brutal kind of fighting. It wasn't a sport. It was a skill which was used to attack and kill.

Kano saw judo as a skill. He felt that judo shouldn't rely on strength or weight. He thought a small, light person could fight a big heavy one – and win. However, the sport became tougher and more competitive. The big heavy people usually beat the small, light ones.

Today, there are different weights in judo, like in boxing. From lightweight to heavyweight, you can find an opponent of the right size!

27

Questions and answers

How can I get started in judo?
First, find a club. There may be
one at your local sports centre.
Sometimes there are judo
classes at local schools in the
evenings.

Are there lots of rules in judo?
Judo is a fighting sport and
people can easily get hurt. So,
yes, there are rules. There are
also the traditions which have
come from Japan. You bow to
your instructor, and to your
opponent, just as in karate.

Then there are practical rules.
• You don't step on the mats
in shoes. Remember that
people are going to end up
face down on those mats!
When you come off the mat
you put your shoes on
immediately. Most **judoka**
(people who do judo) wear
rubber flip-flops.

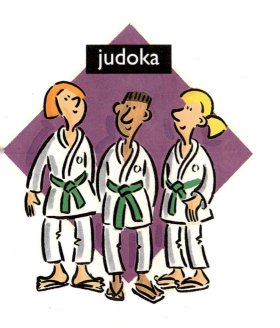

judoka

• You don't wear jewellery, or leave long hair loose. Jewellery can hurt an opponent. Long, loose hair can get caught up in the action.

Can you get hurt doing judo?
Yes, you can. You have to learn to fall easily. Until you do, you can get bruised. Sometimes, there are worse injuries. People dislocate shoulders, and you can break an arm or leg. This is why the warm-up exercises are so important. It's also important not to be impatient. Your instructor knows best how fast you can go.

29

The big six throws

These are the six throws which nearly every judoka (person who does judo) uses.

1 The body drop ▶
This is a hand throw. It is a good one for a beginner to learn. The thrower **(Tori)** jumps in front of the person to be thrown **(Uke)**. She wheels him round his body and over his right foot. Then she drops him.

Tori and Uke

Tori

Uke

2 Both hands shoulder throw ▶

This is another hand throw. He pulls his opponent over his shoulder and holds him down.

◀ **3 Sweeping loin**

This is a one-foot throw. One leg is used to support the thrower and the opponent. The thrower's other leg sweeps the opponent off his feet.

4 Inner thigh

This is another one-foot throw. Here the thrower sweeps the inside of the other's leg. Then she lifts the opponent off the ground and pins him down as he lands.

5 Major outer reaping

The thrower stands beside the opponent and sweeps back with the right leg. This hooks round the opponent's upper right leg. The thrower then brings the opponent down.

6 Stomach throw

This is a sacrifice throw. To do this, the thrower lies on the ground. She pushes her foot into the opponent's stomach. She then pulls the opponent down to the ground over her head.

Club night

Carly is 13. She is a member of a judo club.

How often do you go to judo?

I usually go to the club once a week. Sometimes I go twice a week, if there's a grading coming up and I'm working hard for it.

Are you always keen to go?

Not always. If I'm tired after school or I've got a lot of things to do I don't feel like going. Then I think, there's a grading or a competition coming up. I don't want to lose my ranking. I don't want all the others to catch up with me, so I go. Once I get there, and I'm on the mat, I never wish I hadn't come.

What happens at a session?

Well, first you bow to the teacher. You take your shoes off, of course. And you have to take your watch and jewellery off.

When does the teaching begin?

When you've warmed up, and the teacher's ready. Then we all line up, in grade order. Highest belts are at the top; beginners or white belts are at the bottom.

How do you warm up? Do you do stretching exercises?

You can warm up like that. I usually warm up by going in for throws. That's another way of warming up.

35

What about the beginners?
Do they work with you?

Sort of. The teacher teaches them an easy movement like a throw. Then the advanced ones are shown something more difficult, like a strangle. Then you all work at the movements. If you're a junior and the movements are too easy for you, then you go over and join in with the seniors.

And you're all wearing the proper clothes?

Not the ones who have just started. They usually wear track-suit bottoms and a T-shirt.

Do you do any fighting in the session?

Free fighting, you mean? Yes, after you've worked on the moves. I really like free-fighting. You can do it on your knees – that's ground work, or you can do it standing – that's standing work.

The grading

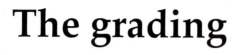

Sam is 15. He is going to explain about gradings.

A grading is when you try for a higher belt. They do some gradings at the club, but usually only the lower gradings.

When you get to higher gradings, you have to go somewhere else. They're quite big events. People come from all over the country. You have to fight someone your own grade. That's why it needs to be a big event, so that there are plenty of people for you to fight.

The first thing you do is get changed. Then you've got to give in your licence. You must have a licence to do a grading. I have a junior licence because I'm under 16. You send away for it, and pay a fee.

Then I have just a little water before I go on the mat, and I usually eat some chocolate to give me energy. I get really nervous before a grading and I feel hot. You're in your age group for a grading. You go on in your group and do a short warm up. Then they call your name out, and your opponent's name.

39

You don't know who you're fighting until then. You usually have three fights, with three different people. They try to match you for size, but if there isn't anyone your grade, then you fight bigger people of a lower grade.

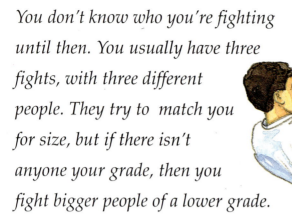

After it's over, you get your licence book back. You look at the back, to see if you've got the next grade. It's a relief when you see you've got it.

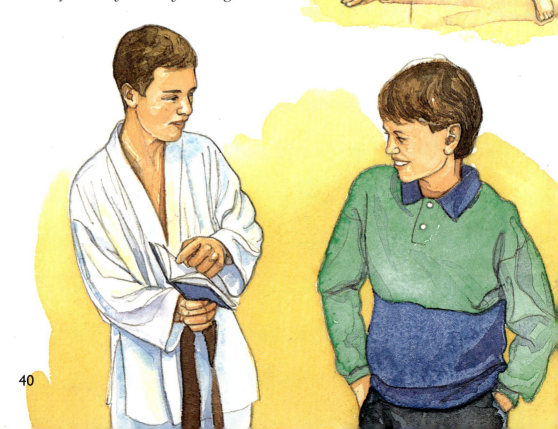

I really like judo. I'm a Brown Belt now, and fourth in the country at my weight. I'm sixteen next year, so I'll

become a senior. I'll have to fight to keep my Brown Belt, and then ... Black Belt here I come!

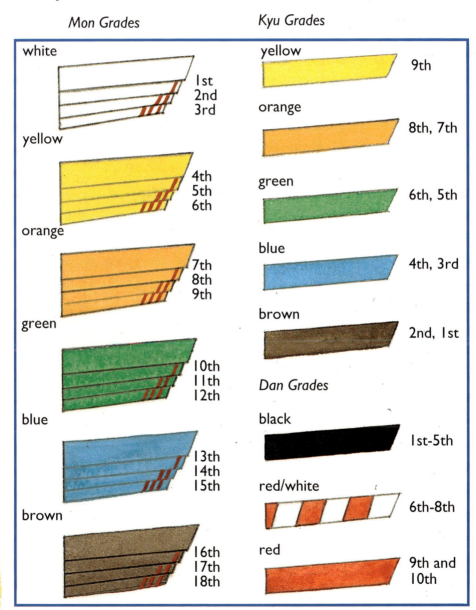

Mon Grades

white — 1st 2nd 3rd

yellow — 4th 5th 6th

orange — 7th 8th 9th

green — 10th 11th 12th

blue — 13th 14th 15th

brown — 16th 17th 18th

Kyu Grades

yellow — 9th

orange — 8th, 7th

green — 6th, 5th

blue — 4th, 3rd

brown — 2nd, 1st

Dan Grades

black — 1st-5th

red/white — 6th-8th

red — 9th and 10th

The champion

One of the greatest of Japan's judo champions was Yasuhiro Yamashita.

Yamashita's fighting weight was 127 kg (280 lbs). He was 1.8 m tall (5ft 11ins). Yamashita fought as a heavyweight.

He was World Champion three times, and Japanese champion eight times. He wasn't beaten in 194 contests.

Yamashita had many offers to turn professional and become a sumo wrestler. He turned them all down. He was determined to win that gold medal!

Yamashita was so strong that he could pick up two 13 year-old boys, one in each hand. Yamashita wanted to win an Olympic medal. He was favourite to win at the Olympic Games in Moscow in 1980. But Japan didn't take part in the Games that year, so he couldn't go.

43

At last it was 1984, and Olympic year again. Yamashita was ready for it. Then, in his first round match he injured his right leg. He could hardly walk. The semi-final was only two hours later.His opponent in the semi-final knew about his injured leg.

He attacked it straight away. This is fair in judo, but it was very painful. Yamashita didn't give in. He saw his opponent was unbalanced. He moved in, and threw him. He held him down – he had won a place in the final.

In the final his opponent was Rashwan, who came from Egypt. Rashwan had won all his earlier rounds with an ippon – the full point for a perfect throw.

Yamashita knew he would have to move quickly, because of his injured leg. He went in for the attack, and in just a few seconds, he had defeated Rashwan. Yamashita bowed to his opponent. He had finally won the Olympic gold medal.

45

Glossary

dojo   The place where you do karate

gi   Suit worn for karate

ippon   A full point in a karate match

judoka   People who do judo

ju-jitsu
and ken-jitsu   Old types of Japanese martial arts

karate chop   Knife hand movement

kata   A group of karate exercises,
                           done in a fixed order

keikio   Karate hand movement.
                           A strike with the finger tips.

koken   Karate hand movement.
                           A strike with the top of the wrist.

kumite	Fighting an opponent in karate
makiwari	A punching post in karate
osu	The word you say in karate when you greet your teacher
seiken	Karate hand movement. A strike with the fist.
shotei	Karate hand movement. A strike with the lower part of the palm.
sokuto	Karate foot movement. A strike with the outside of the foot.
sumo wrestling	Special kind of wrestling in Japan
tameshiwar	Using your bare hand or foot to smash a brick or plank of wood. Tameshiwar means destruction in Japanese.
Tori and Uke	In the body drop in judo, the person throwing is called Tori, the person being thrown is called Uke.

Index